Contents

Projects

General Instructions	2
Christmas Truffles Quilt	4
- Caramel Candies	5
- Perfect Pleasures	6
- Delicious Magnificence	8
- Scrumptious Splendour	10
- Pure Indulgence	11
- Luscious Luxuries	12
- Devine Delicacies	13
- Holly Happiness	14
- Tempting Truffles	16
- Plump Puds	18
- Delectable Delights	21
- Tantalising Treats	22
Putting it all together	23
God Bless Cushion	25
Angel Cushion	26
Christmas Bell Pull	27
Merry Christmas Wallhanging	29
Miracle Stocking	30

Recipes

Christmas Pudding Truffles	7
Double Choc Orange Truffle Balls	13
Marshmallow Surprises	17
Mars Bar Truffles	20
Macadamia Truffles	24
Chocpeppermint Balls	31

Glossary

Glossary	32

Designs by Helen Stubbings
Artwork by Katey McConachy
Photography by Richard Barren

Stubbings, Helen, 1967- .
Christmas truffles.
ISBN 0 9757444 0 2.
1. Patchwork quilts. 2. Stitches (Sewing).
3. Cookery (Truffles). I. McConachy, Katey.
II. Barren, Richard. III. Title.
746.46

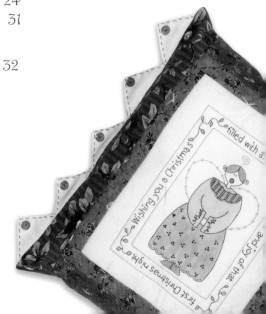

First Things First

General Instructions

- All seams throughout the book are $\frac{1}{4}$". Seam allowances are included in the sizes given in the cutting instructions.
- Requirements given are based on 100% cotton fabric, non-directional, 42" or 110cm wide. Every project in this book has been made with just eight fat eighths of coloured fabrics and 1$\frac{1}{2}$ metres /60 inches of background fabric (not including backings) however individual requirements are given at the beginning of each project.
- Cutting instructions are for 'reds', 'greens' or 'background' only. Follow photographs to choose where to use each fabric. Basically if you 'mix' them up evenly across the project you will have a balanced but scrappy look. You may prefer to use just one of each colour or to use many more than four of each. Either way it will still look good!
- The projects are easiest cut and most accurately made using a rotary blade cutter, ruler and cutting mat. Templates may be made if you do not have this equipment.
- Fabrics are placed right sides together unless otherwise stated in the project instructions.
- I have used a lightweight fusible pellon (very thin batting) behind all of my stitcheries throughout the book. (Note that in the quilt, pellon is applied to the back of the whole block.) This gives a lovely quilted effect and hides any knots or travelling of threads behind the fabric. Check manufacturer's instructions for usage but generally a warm to hot dry iron is used to fuse the layers together. Place the fabric on top of the pellon with the glue dots or rough side uppermost. Press from the fabric side. Use an appliqué mat or pressing mat to protect your iron and your stitchery. You may choose not to use it or instead hand or glue baste a non fusible pellon.
- Read through all instructions before beginning a project.

Order of work

Unless otherwise stated make the projects in the following order:

- Cut all pieces for project
- Trace stitchery. Colour if desired. (see Colourqué™ instructions below)
- Fuse pellon. Stitch. Seal if washing article.
- Make up project as per directions.

Sew and flip method (s/f)

Draw a diagonal pencil line on back of the coloured fabric square. Lay right sides together onto the background piece. Stitch on the drawn line. Press the applicable corner back onto itself. Carefully trim the middle layer of fabric away leaving the $\frac{1}{4}$" seam allowance to lessen the bulk if desired.

Tracing - use a light box, window or light source and a soft mechanical lead pencil or blue water erasable pen (only if you are not colouring). Tape the design (you will have to photocopy this from the book first) onto your light source. Centre the background fabric over the design, tape to secure. Carefully trace the design. You may not need to trace every little detail. For example a line for a leaf or a dot for a flower may suffice and then follow your book as you stitch.

Colourqué™ - use sharp Derwent Artist or Studio pencils to add colour where desired or follow the photographs. It may help to fuse a piece of 'freezer paper' onto the back of the stitchery piece to stabilise whilst colouring. Colour quite darkly as the colour will 'rub off' whilst stitching. After stitching carefully seal the colour in with a small round brush and a textile medium if you intend washing the article. Do not get the medium onto the background fabric as it may stain.

Stitching - use 1 or 2 strands of DMC stranded cotton following the photograph for colour placement or choose your own colours. A size 7 or 8 crewel needle to stitch and a 6-8" embroidery hoop is recommended. Place the fabric into the hoop having the fabric firm but not stretched. Use the stitch guide below for assistance with the individual stitches. Begin and end with knots, as the pellon will 'hide' any threads on the back of your stitchery.

Backstitch	French knot	Running stitch	Detached chain

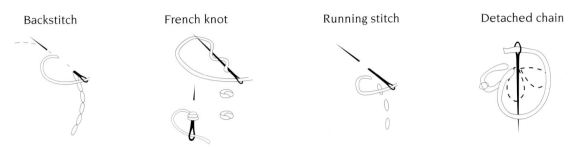

Layering your quilt - press your backing fabric and quilt top carefully. Lay backing fabric right side down onto a table or flat surface. Tape the edges to secure the backing fabric having it taut but not stretched. Smooth your wadding centrally over the backing fabric and then lay the quilt top centrally on to the top. The backing fabric and wadding should be larger than the quilt top by about 1"/2.5cm on all sides. Do not trim it at this stage as you want a full binding. Smooth out any wrinkles and pin or hand baste the three layers together. Or you may like to use your own preferred method of layering.

Quilting your quilt or project
Once your project is layered and secured with pins, basting thread or basting spray you can now quilt it. Use a walking foot for straight line quilting and a darning foot for free motion quilting. You can use matching threads, contrasting threads, invisible threads or specialty threads to quilt. Quilt a long stabilising row in each direction first. Then complete any straight line quilting before ending with free motion quilting such as stippling or meandering to fill sections. Secure the beginnings and endings of all threads.

Binding - in all of the projects I have cut binding strips 2½" wide on the straight grain of the fabric to give a finished ½" double bind. Join your strips to make one long strip. It is best to use mitred joins to lessen the bulk. Press your binding strips in half wrong sides together to give a double layer. Use a ¼" machine foot and attach to the right side of your quilt top mitring the corners. Have the binding edges level with the edges of the quilt top, not the wadding or backing fabric which is larger. Join the start and finish with a mitred join also to lessen bulk and hide the join. Trim corners and the edge of the wadding and backing to ½" from the stitching line. Turn the binding to the back of the quilt, pin and slipstitch covering the stitching line, using a thread which matches the backing fabric.

Mitred joins
Fold all your strips in half with short ends together and lay them on a straight line on your cutting mat with the ends crossing the 45° line. Cut off all ends at the 45° angle.

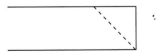

Place two strip ends right sides together and stitch with a ¼" seam taking care not to stretch the bias seam.

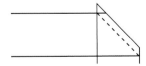

Hanging sleeve
Whether a small or large wallhanging or quilt it is always easier to attach a hanging sleeve before you bind it. Cut a strip of fabric approximately 6" wide and the same width as your finished quilt. Turn in a double hem at both short ends and stitch. Press the strip in half wrong sides together and then position with raw edges even along the top of the back of your quilt. Baste. When attaching the binding to the front you will secure the sleeve in this stitch line. After handstitching the binding to the back of your quilt you can handstitch the sleeve along the bottom edge with the stitch going through the backing fabric only.

Christmas Truffles

Quilt measures 80cm/32" x 78cm/31"

Requirements for Christmas Truffles quilt

A - background fabric - 1metre/40"

B - greens - four fat eighths

C - reds - four fat eighths

Border - 15cm/6" red, 15cm/6" light background

Binding - 1/2m/20" or leftover strips of your red fabrics

Fusible pellon - 1m/40"

DMC Stranded cotton - Variegated Garnet 115, Very Dark Pistachio Green 319

Derwent Artist pencil #1900 Madder Carmine

Fabric guide

A - background stitchery fabric

B - four assorted greens

C - four assorted reds

All given measurements are cutting measurements and include ¼" seam allowance. Cut pieces as instructed and follow diagram and photograph to piece. Use the sew and flip method as shown in the General Instructions where indicated. Use a ¼" sewing machine foot and 100% cotton sewing thread.

Order of work

• Cut and piece each block following the instructions for each section.

• Trace the corresponding stitchery design onto the background fabric pieces in each section.

• Colour where indicated if desired following the Colourqué™ technique given under General Instructions.

• Fuse pellon to the back of the whole block and then stitch.

Stitching - use 1 or 2 strands of DMC stranded cotton following the diagram for colour placement or choose your own colours to match your chosen fabrics. A #7 or #8 crewel needle to stitch and a 6-8" hoop is recommended. Place the block into the hoop having the fabric firm but not stretched. Use the stitch guide under General instructions for assistance with the individual stitches. All work in the quilt is stitched using only backstitch, running stitch, detached chain stitch and French knots.

Colourqué™

Colour all stripes and large cherries using a sharp Derwent Artists #1900 pencil. You can also add a little colour to Santa's nose.

1. Caramel Candies

Fabric a (background) - cut 1 @ 4 $\frac{1}{2}$" x 3$\frac{1}{2}$" - candy cane

  - cut 1@12$\frac{1}{2}$" x 2$\frac{1}{2}$" - three angels

Fabric b (greens) - cut 2@1$\frac{1}{2}$" x 3$\frac{1}{2}$"

Fabric c (reds) - cut 2@1$\frac{1}{2}$" x 6$\frac{1}{2}$"

• Attach fabric b strips to top and bottom of stitchery, press

• Attach fabric c strips to both sides, press

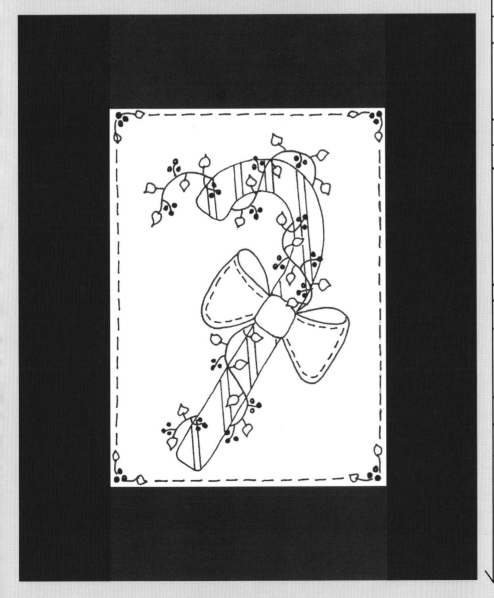

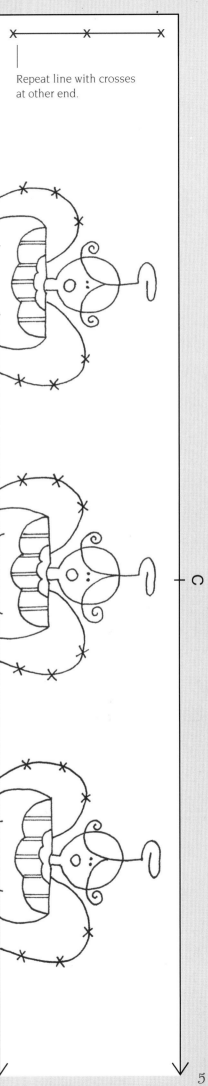

Repeat line with crosses at other end.

C

Christmas Truffles cont.

2. Perfect Pleasures

Fabric a (background)	- cut 1@5$\frac{1}{2}$" x 4$\frac{1}{2}$" - wreath
	- cut 16@2$\frac{1}{2}$" x 2$\frac{1}{2}$" - vine
Fabric c (reds)	- cut 8@1$\frac{1}{2}$" x 1$\frac{1}{2}$" s/f

Fabric b (greens)	- cut 4@2$\frac{1}{2}$" x 2$\frac{1}{2}$" s/f
	- cut 24@1$\frac{1}{2}$" x 1$\frac{1}{2}$" s/f

• Sew and flip a large green square to two diagonally opposite corners of the large background piece. Press and repeat with the remaining two large green squares. Press.

• Sew and flip a small green square to opposite corners of eight background squares. Press.

• Sew and flip one green square and one red square to opposite corners of remaining background squares.

• Join these units into two rows of six squares, and two rows of two squares following the diagram for colour placement. Press seams to the right on one row and to the left on the other.

• Match and pin seams and stitch the two long rows and two short rows together. Press well. Do not join them all up at this stage. This will make sense in the 'putting it all together' stage.

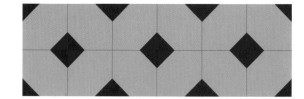

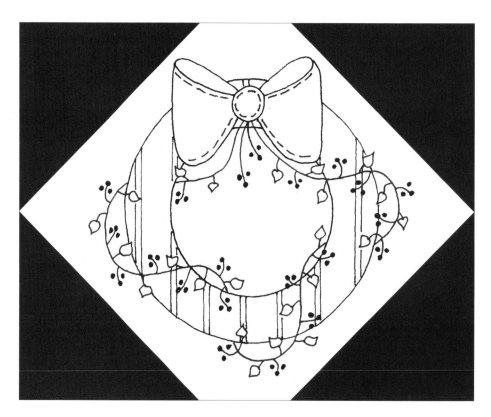

Christmas Pudding Truffles

Linda Thompson-Young

Makes approx. 70 puds

Ingredients

800g/28oz packaged readymade dark fruitcake

$^1/_2$ cup brandy

White chocolate melts

*Green spearmint leaves - approx 12

*Red raspberries or jube lollies - approx 6

* see Glossary

Method

Crumble the cake into a bowl and sprinkle the brandy over. Mix well together.

Take heaped teaspoons of the mix and roll into balls. Place on a tray and refrigerate.

Cut the raspberries and spearmint leaves with kitchen scissors. Then squeeze 2 pieces of spearmint and 1 piece of raspberry together to resemble sprigs of holly.

Melt the chocolate (Linda uses a small snaplock bag to melt them in the microwave on medium for approximately 1 minute. Then cut off one corner and use the bag like a piping bag). Drizzle chocolate over the mini puddings and decorate with the holly sprigs. Store in refrigerator.

Christmas Truffles cont.

3. Delicious Magnificence

Fabric a (background)
- cut 1@10½" x 3½"- stars
- cut 3@4½" x 3½"- tree
- cut 2@1½" x 1½" - sprays

Fabric c (reds)
- cut 4@ 2½" x 2½" s/f

Fabric b (greens)
- cut 2@2½" x 2½" s/f
- cut 2@1½" x 1½"

- Join green and background small squares alternately. Press to green.

- Sew and flip a red square to the top right of two background rectangles. Press. Sew the remaining two red squares to the top left of each rectangle. Press. Do the same with the green squares and remaining background rectangle.

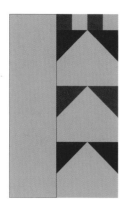

- Join three units as per the diagram and attach your small square strip to the top. Press seams upwards.
- Attach the large background piece to the left side of your block.

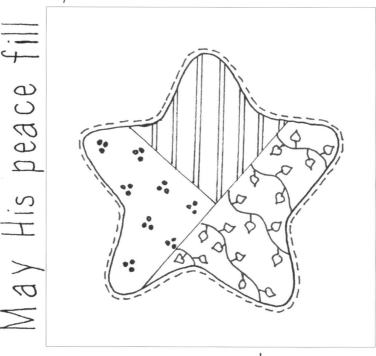

your home and His

May His peace fill

joy shine upon the

ones you love

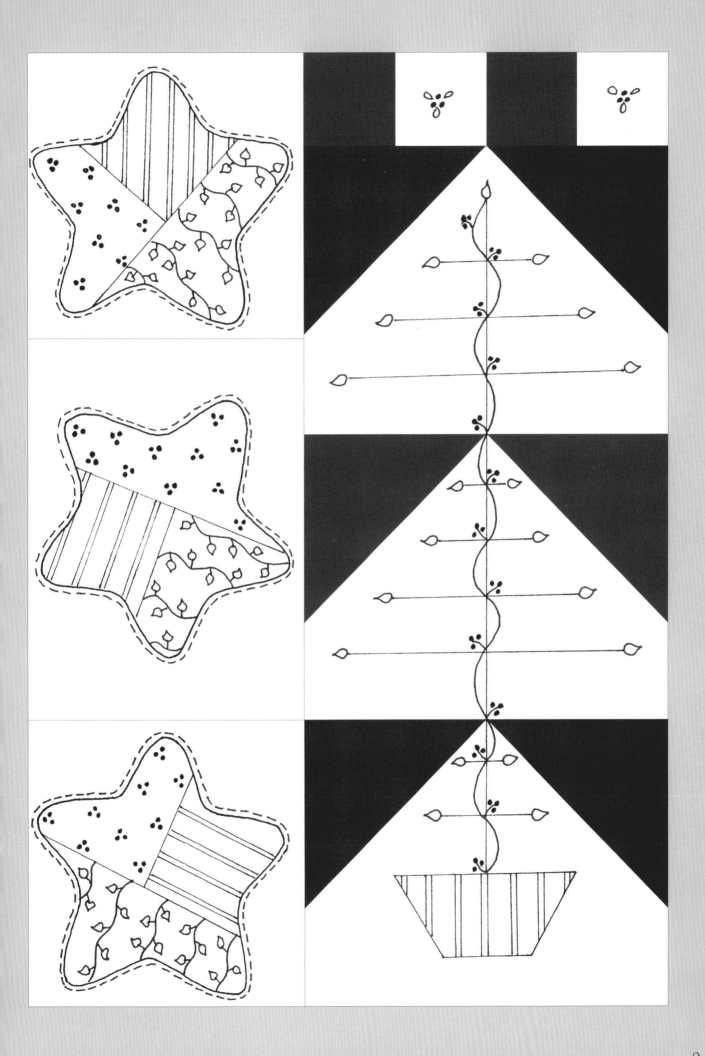

Christmas Truffles cont.

4. Scrumptious Splendour

Fabric a
(background)   - cut 1@12½" x 4½"- trees
              - cut 18@1½" x 1½" - sprays
Fabric c (reds) - cut 18@1½" x 1½"

• Join small red and background squares to make: two rows of four and two rows of 14. Press all seams towards the red squares.

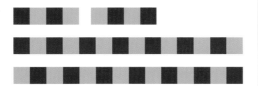

• Join the two short rows and the two long rows together matching the seams.

• Attach the short unit to the end of the large background piece.

• Attach the long unit to the bottom. Press well.

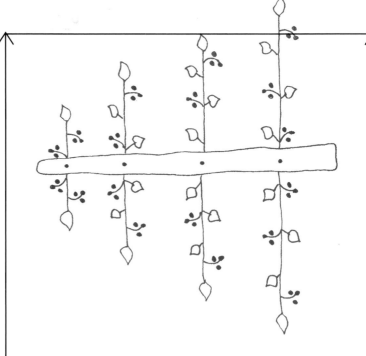

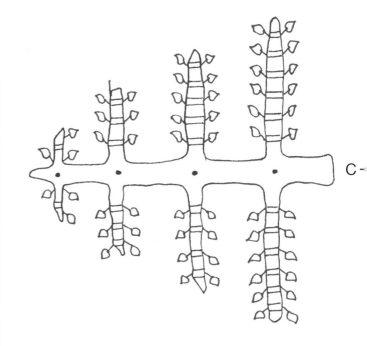

C -

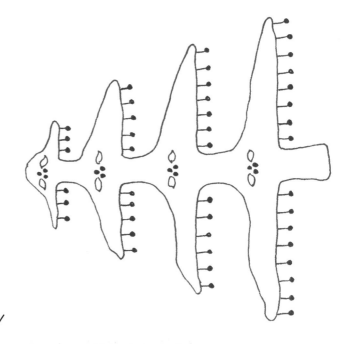

5. Pure Indulgence

Fabric a (background) - cut 1@8$\frac{1}{2}$" x 3$\frac{1}{2}$" - hearts

Fabric b (greens) - cut 2@ 8$\frac{1}{2}$" x 2$\frac{1}{2}$"

• Attach green strip to top and
  bottom of background strip.
  Press seams towards green.

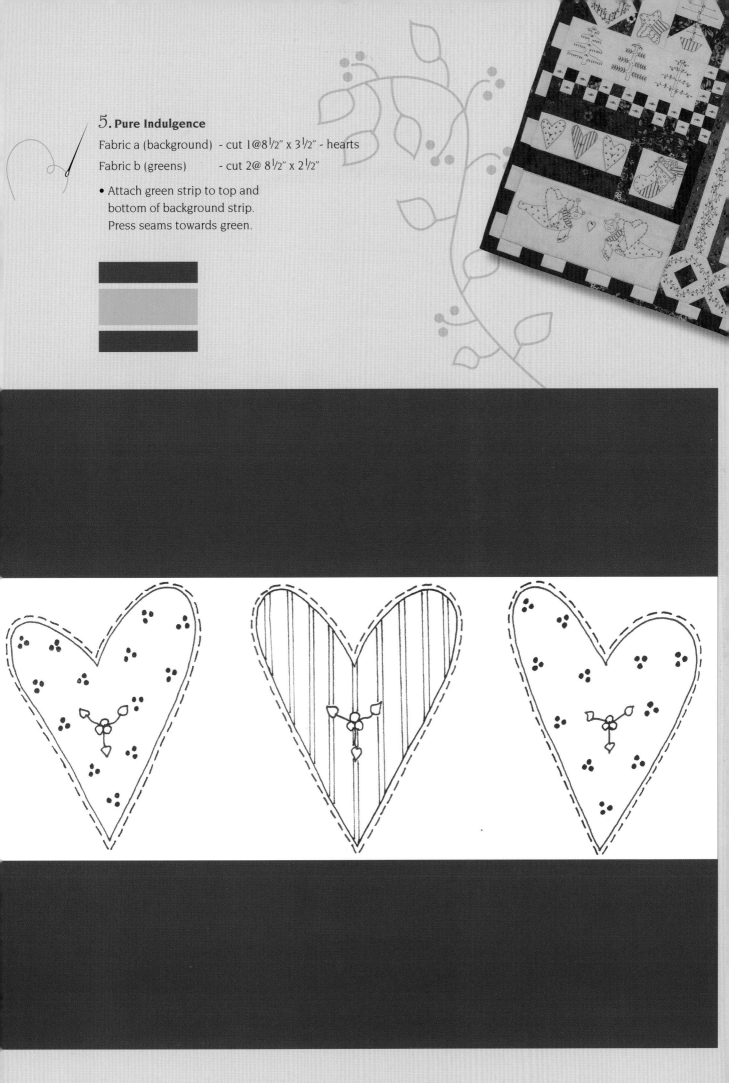

6. Luscious Luxuries

Fabric a (background) - cut 1@4$\frac{1}{2}$" x 4$\frac{1}{2}$" - stocking

Fabric b (greens) - cut 2@ 4$\frac{1}{2}$" x 1$\frac{1}{2}$"

Fabric c (reds) - cut 1@6$\frac{1}{2}$" x 1$\frac{1}{2}$"
- cut 1@7$\frac{1}{2}$" x 1$\frac{1}{2}$"
- cut 1@5$\frac{1}{2}$" x 1$\frac{1}{2}$"

• Attach a green strip to the top and bottom of your background piece. Press seams to green.

• Attach the red 6 $\frac{1}{2}$" strip to the left side. Press seam outwards.

• Attach 5 $\frac{1}{2}$" red strip to the top.
  Press seam outwards.

• Attach remaining red strip to
  right side of block. Press.

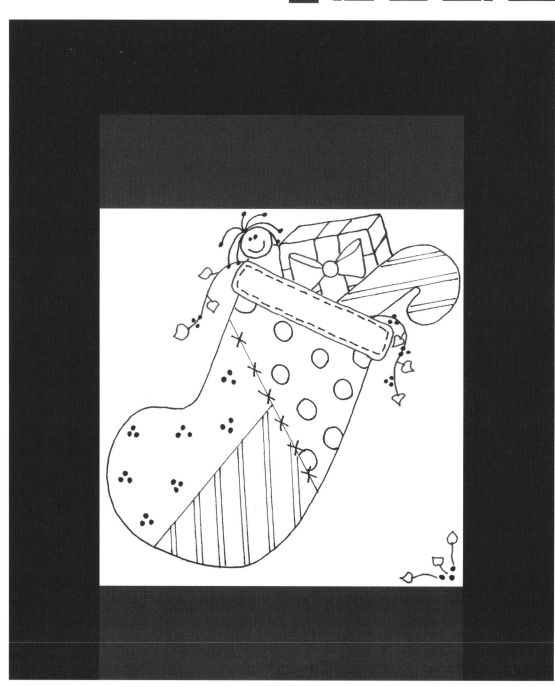

Love was born at Christmas; Star and angels gave the sign

Double Choc Orange Truffle Balls

*250g/8oz crushed sweet biscuits
3⁄4 cup desiccated coconut
4 tablespoons cocoa
395g/14oz can sweetened condensed milk
2 tablespoons Grand Marnier or orange liqueur
extra coconut or chocolate shavings for rolling in.

Mix all ingredients. Refrigerate until firm. Shape into balls; roll in coconut or chocolate shavings. Refrigerate.

* see Glossary

7. Devine Delicacies

Fabric a (background)
- cut 1 @ 14$\frac{1}{2}$" x 6$\frac{1}{2}$" - angels

Place on centre mark of background fabric.
Trace and then flip for other side.

C

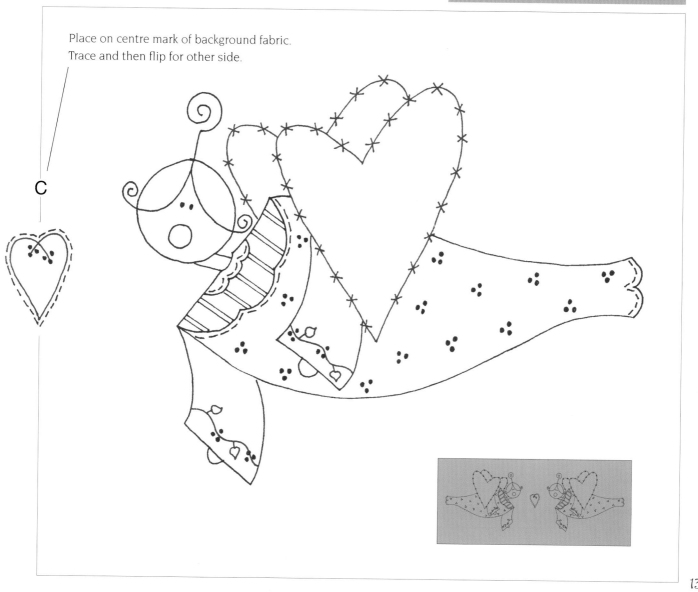

8. Holly Happiness

Fabric a (background)   - cut 1@4$\frac{1}{2}$" x 4$\frac{1}{2}$"- holly   Fabric b (greens)   - cut 8@ 2$\frac{1}{2}$" x 2$\frac{1}{2}$" s/f
                         - cut 8@2$\frac{1}{2}$" x 2$\frac{1}{2}$" - hearts and sprays   - cut 2@ 4$\frac{1}{2}$" x 1$\frac{1}{2}$"

Fabric c (reds)   - cut 1@2$\frac{1}{2}$" x 2$\frac{1}{2}$"
                     - cut 4@1$\frac{1}{2}$" x 1$\frac{1}{2}$" s/f

- Sew and flip a green square to one side of eight background squares.
- Sew and flip a red square to opposite corner of four of these units.

- Join as a nine patch block following diagram for layout and pressing seams in opposite directions.

- Attach a green strip to either side of background rectangle. Press to green.

- Attach two units together.

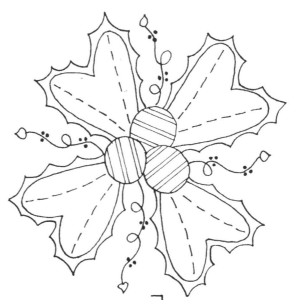

May the Blessings of

Peace and Happiness

fill your home

9. Tempting Truffles

Fabric a (background)	- cut 1@4½" x 3½" - bells	
	- cut 4@3½" x 3½"- baubles and hearts	
Fabric b (greens)	- cut 2@ 4½" x 1½"	Fabric c (reds)
	- cut 4@ 2½" x 2½" s/f	
	- cut 1@ 6½" x 1½"	

Fabric c (reds) - cut 1@6½" x 1½"
- cut 1@ 4½" x 1½"
- cut 4@2½" x 2½" s/f

- Attach 4 ½" red strip to right of background rectangle. Press to red.
- Attach 4 ½" green strips to top and bottom. Press to green.
- Attach red 6 ½" strip to left and green 6 ½" to right of block. Press outwards.

- Sew and flip a green square to diagonally opposite corners of two background squares.
- Sew and flip red squares to remaining opposite corners.

- Join these units with remaining background squares to make a four patch. Press seams to background. Attach four patch to the right side of your bell unit.

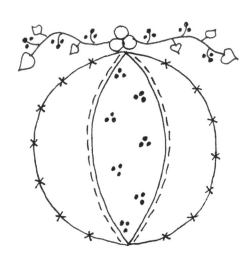

Marshmallow Surprises
from Lynette Wallbridge

Ingredients

*250g/8oz plain sweet biscuits - crushed

200g/7oz marshmallows - chopped

200g/7oz dried apricots - chopped

1 cup crushed nuts

395g/14oz can sweetened condensed milk

1/2 cup desiccated coconut

*150g/5oz white or milk chocolate

Method

Mix all ingredients together except coconut into bowl with hands. Sprinkle coconut onto foil and lay mixture in long strip onto coconut. Sprinkle more coconut on top. Roll up foil to form a tight log. Refrigerate until firm.

Unwrap logs and cut into 1cm slices. Melt white chocolate in double saucepan. Drizzle melted chocolate or use a piping bag to pipe chocolate onto slices.

Alternatively press mixture into lined tray. Drizzle with melted chocolate and cut into bars to serve when firm.

* see Glossary

May the quiet and gentle that first morning be today ... peace love of Christmas yours and always...

Christmas Truffles cont.

10. Plump Puds

Fabric a (background)   - cut 1@9$\frac{1}{2}$" x 6$\frac{1}{2}$" - angel
                              - cut 9@2$\frac{1}{2}$" x 2$\frac{1}{2}$"-pudding, holly and hearts

Fabric b (greens)   - cut 12@1$\frac{1}{2}$" x 1$\frac{1}{2}$" s/f   Fabric c (reds)   - cut 8@1$\frac{1}{2}$" x 1$\frac{1}{2}$" s/f

- Sew and flip a green square to two diagonally opposite corners of four background squares.
- Sew and flip a third green square to each of these background squares.

- Sew and flip a red square to four background squares. Repeat with a second red square.

- Join your patches as a nine patch block as per diagram placing the remaining background square into the centre.

 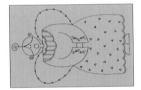

Mars Bar Truffles

Virginia Purdey

85g/3oz butter
*3 x 60g/2oz Mars Bars
*3 cups rice bubbles
*375g/13oz packet
  dark chocolate melts

Melt butter and mars bars in saucepan on low heat. Stir in rice bubbles. Refrigerate until almost set. Roll mixture into balls. Refrigerate again until set.

Melt chocolate in double saucepan. Dip balls into melted chocolate and place on baking paper on tray in fridge until set.

*see Glossary

Place on centre mark of background fabric.
Trace and then flip for other end.

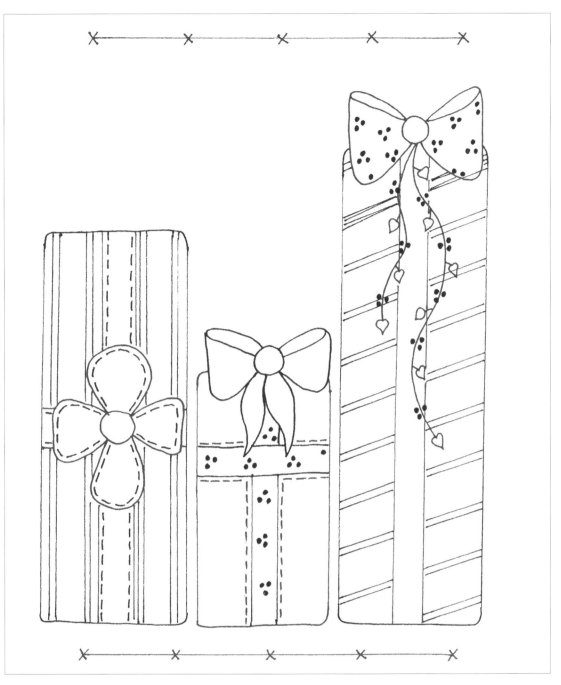

11. Delectable Delights

Fabric a (background)   - cut 1@7$\frac{1}{2}$" x 6$\frac{1}{2}$" - presents
                        - cut 1@2$\frac{1}{2}$" x 15$\frac{1}{2}$" - ribbon vine
                        - cut 3@1$\frac{1}{2}$" x 1$\frac{1}{2}$" - sprays

Fabric b (greens)   - cut 2@1$\frac{1}{2}$" x 15$\frac{1}{2}$"
                        - cut 3@1$\frac{1}{2}$" x1$\frac{1}{2}$"

- Join three green squares and three background squares together alternately. Press seams to green.

- Attach strip to small background rectangle.

- Join a long green strip to either side of background strip. Press to green.

Christmas Truffles cont.

12. Tantalising Treats

Fabric a (background)
- cut 1@4$\frac{1}{2}$" x 11$\frac{1}{2}$" - Santa
- cut 1@1$\frac{1}{2}$" x 2$\frac{1}{2}$"- spray
- cut 16@1$\frac{1}{2}$" x 1$\frac{1}{2}$"

Fabric b (greens) - cut 2@1$\frac{1}{2}$" x 2$\frac{1}{2}$"
Fabric c (reds)   - cut 16@1$\frac{1}{2}$" x 1$\frac{1}{2}$" s/f

• Sew and flip 16 red and background squares.
• Join together in fours to make pinwheels.
• Join two sets of two pinwheels.

 • Attach green strip to both sides of small background rectangle. Press to green.

• Attach pinwheel pairs to either side to make one long pieced strip. Press to green.

• Attach remaining background rectangle to right hand side. Press to background.

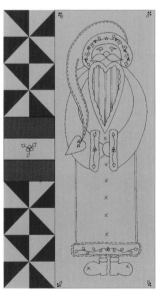

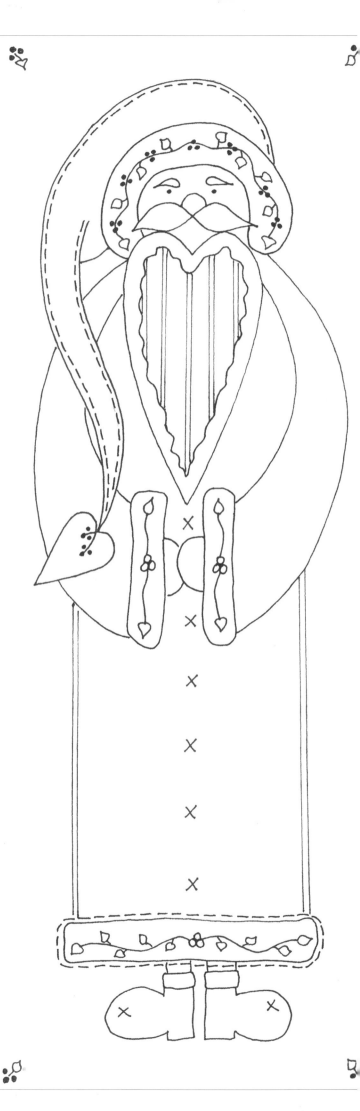

Putting it all Together

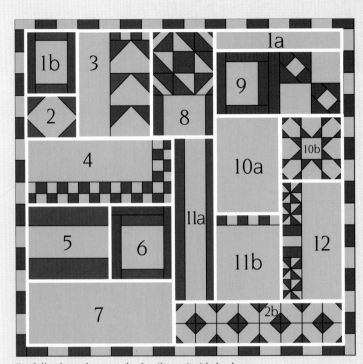

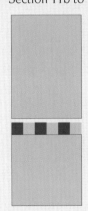

For full colour photograph of quilt see inside back cover.

Once all sections are stitched, sealed and completed you need to put them all together to form your quilt. Following the sectioned diagram join the following:

Section 1b to 2 = A

Section 5 to 6 = B

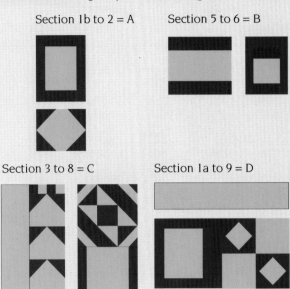

Section 3 to 8 = C

Section 1a to 9 = D

Section 10b to 12 = E

Section 11b to 10a = F

Section A to C = G

Join 4 to B to 7 = H

Join G to H = I - You need to stop ¼" from the top right corner of H to allow 'setting in' of next section

Join single section 2b unit to bottom of 11a.

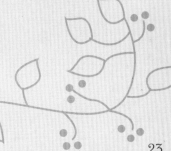

Insert 11a to I = J

Join E to F = K

Join K to D = L   Join L to 2b = M

Join J to M

Clear as mud!!! Follow the diagrams and pictures...

- Final border - cut two strips red fabric 2$\frac{1}{2}$" by width of fabric
- Cut two strips light background fabric 2$\frac{1}{2}$" by width of fabric
- Join dark/light strips together along the length, press seams towards reds
- Cross cut into 1$\frac{1}{2}$" pieces
- Measure quilt and join pieces in pairs to make border strips to fit
- Mark the $\frac{1}{4}$, $\frac{1}{2}$ and $\frac{3}{4}$ points along the sides of your quilt. Do the same on your border strips. Match these points right sides together with raw edges even and pin. Attach using a $\frac{1}{4}$" seam allowance. Repeat for the top and bottom borders.

- Layer, quilt as desired, attach hanging sleeve and bind your quilt. Don't forget to add a label to the back!

Macadamia Truffles

Ingredients

200g/7oz white chocolate

125g/4oz packet Philadelphia cream cheese

1 tablespoon honey

1 teaspoon vanilla essence/extract

20 macadamia nuts

$\frac{1}{4}$ cup desiccated coconut

$\frac{1}{2}$ cup coconut extra for rolling

Method

Melt chocolate in double saucepan.

Beat chocolate, cream cheese, honey and vanilla with an electric beater until smooth. Stir in coconut. Refrigerate until firm.

Roll mixture around macadamia nut to form ball. Roll in extra coconut and refrigerate again.

God Bless Cushion

Requirements

Fabric a (background)	- 18cm/7"	Fabric b (greens)	- 5cm/2"
Fabric c (reds)	- 5cm/2"	Pellon	- 17cm/8"
Cushion back fabric	- 30cm/12" Fibrefill toy stuffing or cushion filler		
DMC stranded cottons	- 115 - Variegated Garnet, 319 - Dark Pistachio Green, 838 - Very Dark Beige Brown		
Derwent Studio pencils	- 19 - Madder Carmine, 43 - Bottle Green, 58 - Raw Sienna		

Cutting

Fabric a (background)	- cut 1 @ 6$\frac{1}{2}$" x 6$\frac{1}{2}$" - stitchery	Fabric b (greens)	- cut 2 @ 2" x 7$\frac{1}{2}$"
	- cut 12 @ 1$\frac{1}{2}$" x 1$\frac{1}{2}$" s/f		- cut 2 @ 2" x 11$\frac{1}{2}$"
Fabric c (reds)	- cut 12 @ 1$\frac{1}{2}$" x 1$\frac{1}{2}$" s/f		
	- cut 2 @ 1" x 8$\frac{1}{2}$"		

• Sew and flip 12 red and background squares to make 12 half square triangle units. Join to make two rows of six units. Press seams in one direction. • Attach to the top and bottom of your stitchery panel. Press to panel.

• Attach red strips to sides of stitchery panel. Press to red. • Attach short green strips to top and bottom. Press to green. • Attach remaining green strips to sides. Press to green.

God bless you with the gentle spirit

Christmas brings and all the season's lovely things!

• Lay panel right sides together with cushion backing. Trim to match. Stitch around outside edge with a $\frac{1}{4}$" seam leaving a 3" opening on one side. Clip corners, turn through and press.

• Using a matching sewing thread stitch a line $\frac{1}{2}$" from outside edge again leaving an opening alongside the previous one. Tie off ends neatly. Stuff firmly then finish your line of stitching again tying off ends neatly. Slipstitch opening closed.

Angel Cushion

Requirements

Fabric a (background)	- 15cm/6"
Fabric c (reds)	- 5cm/2"
Cushion back fabric	- 23cm x 30cm/9" x 12"

Fabric b (greens) - 3cm/1"
Pellon - 15cm x 19cm/6" x 7$\frac{1}{2}$"
Fibrefill toy stuffing or cushion filling

DMC stranded cotton threads - 115 - Variegated Garnet, 319 - Very Dark Pistachio Green, 729 - Medium Old Gold, 322 - Dark Dark Baby Blue, 838 - Very Dark Beige Brown

Derwent studio pencils - 19 - Madder Carmine, 29 - Ultramarine, 43 - Bottle Green, 59 - Golden Brown, 61 - Copper Beech

10 x 6mm/$\frac{1}{4}$" red buttons

Cutting

Fabric a (background) - cut 1 @ 6" x 7$\frac{1}{2}$" - stitchery
　　　　　　　　　　　 - cut 10 @ 2$\frac{1}{2}$" x 2$\frac{1}{2}$" - prairie points

Fabric c (reds)　　　　 - cut 2 @ 2" x 7"
　　　　　　　　　　　 - cut 2 @ 2" x 11$\frac{1}{2}$"

Fabric b (greens) - cut 2 @ 1" x 7"
　　　　　　　　　　- cut 2 @ 1" x 7$\frac{1}{2}$"

- Attach 7$\frac{1}{2}$" green strips to sides of stitchery. Press to green • Attach remaining green strips to top and bottom of stitchery. Press to green. • Attach 7" red strips to top and bottom of stitchery panel. Press to red.

- Attach remaining red strips to sides. Press to red.

- Fold and press background squares twice diagonally to form prairie points. Position five evenly along each side overlapping where necessary and having raw edges even. Leave $\frac{1}{4}$" gap at either end so they do not get caught in seam. Baste.

- Lay panel right sides together with backing fabric. Trim edges to match and stitch around outside edge with a $\frac{1}{4}$" seam leaving a 2 - 3" opening on one side behind prairie points. Clip corners, turn through opening and press.

- Stuff evenly with fibrefill and slip stitch opening closed.

- Stitch a running stitch around the edge of the prairie points and attach a button to each one as per photograph.

filled with all the

Wishing you a Christmas

wonder and joy of that

first Christmas night

Christmas Bell Pull

Requirements

Fabric a (background) - 20cm/8"	Fabric b (greens) - 20cm/8"
Fabric c (reds)	- 5cm/2"

Fusible pellon - 30cm/12"   Backing fabric - 30cm/12"

DMC stranded thread - 115 - Variegated Garnet
Derwent Studio pencil - 19 - Madder Carmine

2 x 6mm/$\frac{1}{4}$" red buttons

Cutting

Fabric a (background) - cut 2 @ 6$\frac{1}{2}$" x 6$\frac{1}{2}$" - stitcheries
                              - cut 2 @ 4" x 2" - hangers

Fabric b (greens) - cut 1 @ 12" x 5" - point
                         - cut 6 @ 4" x 2$\frac{1}{2}$"
                         - cut 10 @ 4$\frac{1}{2}$" x 2$\frac{1}{2}$"

Fabric c (reds) - cut 2 @ 1" x 6$\frac{1}{2}$"
                 - cut 2 @ 1" x 7$\frac{1}{2}$"

- Attach a short red strip to the top and bottom of each stitchery piece. Press to red.

- Attach remaining strips to both sides of stitchery pieces. Press to red.

- Join 6 smaller green rectangles into pairs.

- Attach a green pair to the top of each stitchery panel and to the bottom of the bottom panel. Join the two panels.

- Join remaining green rectangles into two strips of five pieces. Press in one direction. Attach one to either side of your stitchery panels.

- Fold large green rectangle in half and mark the centre point. Draw a line from each corner to this point. Cut on line. Attach triangle to bottom of your stitchery panel.

- Sew small background strips in half along the long side. Turn through. Press seam to centre. Fold in half with the seam to the inside and position along top of hanging with raw edges even. Baste into position.

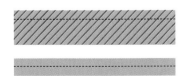

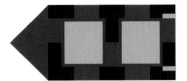

- Lay entire hanging onto glue side of fusible pellon. Trim outer edges to match and fuse. Lay right sides onto backing fabric; again trim to match outer edges. Stitch entire outside edge with $\frac{1}{4}$" seam leaving a 3" opening on one side. Trim corners, turn through opening and press well. Slipstitch opening closed.

- Attach a red button to each hanging loop if desired as per photograph.

Christmas Bell Pull cont.

May the miracle of that first Christmas fill your heart with joy ~ Joy

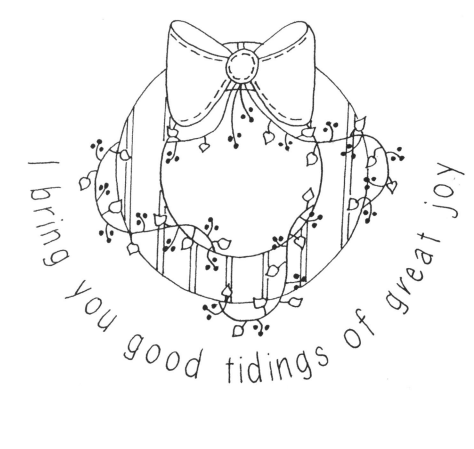

I bring you good tidings of great joy

Merry Christmas Wallhanging

Requirements

Fabric a (background) - 10cm/4"
Fabric c (reds) - 5cm/2"
Pellon, backing fabric - 23cm x 18cm/9" x 7"

DMC stranded cotton thread

- 115 Variegated Garnet

3 x 6mm/$\frac{1}{4}$" red buttons
2 x 8mm/$\frac{3}{8}$" red buttons

Cutting

Fabric a (background) -cut 1 @ 4" x 6" - stitchery
           - cut 2 @ 2" x 4" - hangers
           - cut 3 @ 2$\frac{1}{2}$" x 2$\frac{1}{2}$"
            (prairie points)

Fabric c (reds) - cut 2 @ 1$\frac{1}{2}$" x 6"
           - cut 2 @ 2" x 7"

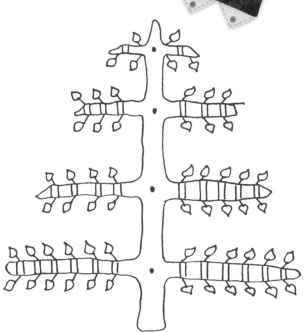

- Attach a 6" red strip to both sides of stitchery. Press to red.

- Attach a 7" red strip to the top and bottom. Press to red.

- Fold and sew background hanging strips along long side. Turn through. Turn seam line to centre and press. Fold in half and evenly place along top of hanging with raw edges even. Baste.

- Press background squares in half diagonally twice to form small triangles. Position evenly along bottom edge of hanging with raw edges even. Leave $\frac{1}{4}$" gap at either end so they do not get caught in seam. Baste.

- Lay hanging wrong side down onto glue side of pellon. Trim edges to match. Fuse.

- Lay right sides together with backing fabric. Sew around outside edge with $\frac{1}{4}$" seam leaving a 2 - 3" opening along bottom edge behind prairie points. Trim corners, turn through and press. Slipstitch opening closed.

- Stitch a running stitch around the edge of the prairie points and the outside of stitchery panel: sew small red buttons as per the photograph. Attach the larger buttons to the hanging loops.

Miracle Stocking

Requirements

Fabric a (background)	- 14cm/5½"
Fabric b (greens) and fabric c (reds)	- various strips 1" - 2" wide to make 5½" x 3½" and 6" x 8½" pieces.
Backing fabric	- 23cm/9"
Pellon	- 14cm x 17cm/5½" x 6½"
DMC stranded cotton	- 115 - Variegated Garnet, 319 - Dark Pistachio Green
Derwent Studio pencil	- 19 - Madder Carmine
4 x 6mm/¼" red buttons	

Cutting

Fabric a (background)	- 1 @ 5½" x 6½" - stitchery
	- 3 @ 2½" x 2½" - prairie points
	- 1 @ 2" x 8½"
	- 1 @ 2" x 4" - hanging loop
	- 1 @ 2" x 10½" - facing
Fabric b & c (reds and greens)	- approx seven strips @ 1 - 2" x 8½"
	- approx four strips @ 1 - 2" x 5½"

- Join short red and green strips to make a piece approximately 5½" x 3½". Press in one direction.

- Join long red, green and background strips to make a piece approximately 6" x 8½". Press in one direction.

- Trace and cutout toe template. Lay onto larger strip piece and mark. Cut on marked line. Attach this piece to the bottom of your stitchery. Press to strips.

- Attach smaller strip piece to top of stitchery. Press to strips.

- Lay stocking right sides together with backing fabric. Pin and stitch around outside edge with ¼" seam leaving the top open. Trim extra fabric back to match. Clip corners, turn through and press well.

- Fold and press background squares twice diagonally to make prairie points. Position evenly along front top of stocking with raw edges even. Baste.

- Fold and sew background hanging strips along long side. Turn through. Turn seam line to centre and press. Fold in half and position on side seam of stocking with raw edges even. Baste.

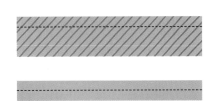

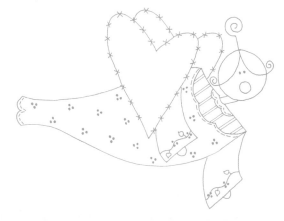

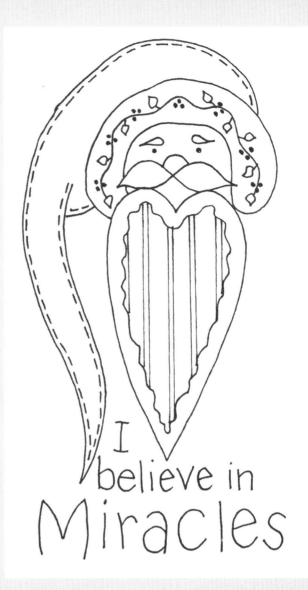

I believe in Miracles

- Turn a double ¼" on long edge of remaining background fabric strip. Edgestitch. Sew right sides together along the short sides to form a tube. Place over top of stocking, right sides together with the seam over the hanging loop seam and raw edges even. Stitch around top edge with ¼" seam securing the prairie points and loop as you go. Turn facing to inside and press.

- Stitch a running stitch around the edge of the prairie points and either side of any background colour strips as per the photograph. Attach a button to each prairie point and the hanging loop.

Chocpeppermint Balls

from Linda Thompson-Young

Ingredients

*1- packet Chocolate Ripple biscuits
*2 Nestle 35g/1oz Peppermint Crisps
½ cup desiccated coconut
395g/14oz can sweetened condensed milk
extra coconut to roll balls in or white chocolate

Method

Mix crushed biscuits, crushed peppermint crisps and coconut together. Add condensed milk and mix well.

Refrigerate until firm.

Roll into balls, roll in extra coconut or drizzle white melted chocolate over and chill in fridge. You could also make it into logs, slice and serve

* see Glossary

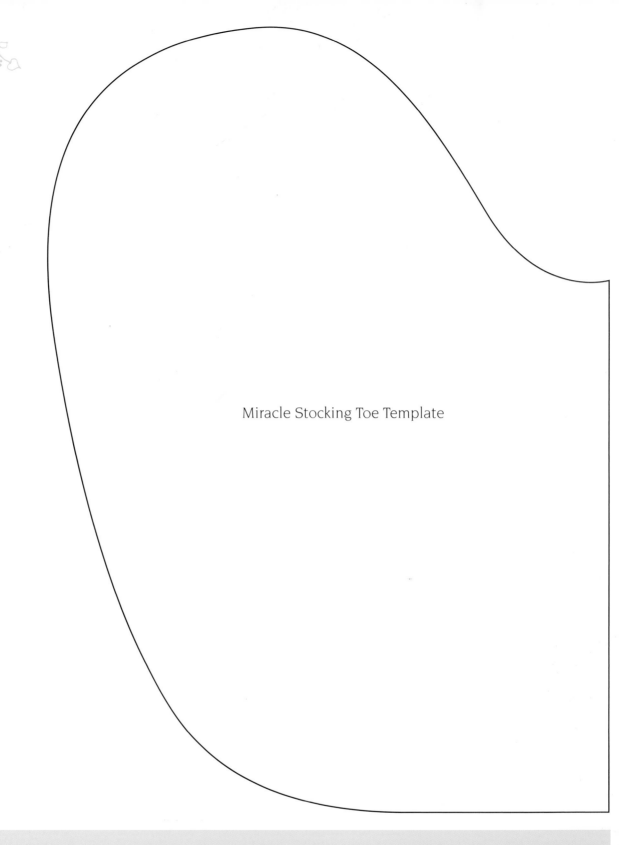

Miracle Stocking Toe Template

Glossary

- Chocolate ripple biscuits 250g/8oz packets - plain chocolate flavoured biscuits/cookies
- Plain sweet biscuits - 250g/8oz packets - Marie biscuits, Milk Arrowroot, Milk Coffee, Graham Crackers, plain cookies.
- Green spearmint leaves –gum confectionary/candy – soft jube mint flavoured covered in sugar, green in colour - substitute green glacé fruit/cherries
- Red raspberries - gum confectionary/candy, red in colour, soft jube - substitute red glace fruit/cherries
- Nestle 35g/1oz Peppermint Crisps - chocolate coated confectionary/candy bar with a crispy mint centre
- Mars Bar - nougat caramel chocolate confectionary/candy bar
- Rice Bubbles - sweetened puffed rice cereal, Rice Krispies
- Chocolate melts - chocolate buds or small pieces suited to melting, available in dark, milk or white flavours